Why Animals Show Off

To the doctors and staff at The Hospital for Sick Children, Toronto — you rock!
— *Peter Cook and Laura Suzuki*

Beauty is all around us. To Joanne, one of the most beautiful things in my life.
— *Love, Ron*

The illustrations for this book were done with paper sculpture and watercolour.
Each layer was cut, formed and painted before being glued into place.

Photography by William Kuryluk.

This book was designed in QuarkXPress, with type set in 16 point Bookman.

Scholastic Canada Ltd.
175 Hillmount Road, Markham, Ontario L6C 1Z7, Canada

Scholastic Inc.
555 Broadway, New York, NY 10012, USA

Scholastic Australia Pty Limited
PO Box 579, Gosford, NSW 2250, Australia

Scholastic New Zealand Limited
Private Bag 94407, Greenmount, Auckland, New Zealand

Scholastic Ltd.
Villiers House, Clarendon Avenue, Leamington Spa,
Warwickshire CV32 5PR, UK

National Library of Canada Cataloguing in Publication

Cook, Peter, 1965-
Why animals show off / Peter Cook, Laura Suzuki ;
illustrated by Ron Broda.

Issued also in French under title: M'as tu vu?
ISBN 0-439-98861-6

1. Animal communication—Juvenile literature. 2. Animal
behavior—Juvenile literature. I. Suzuki, Laura II. Broda, Ron III. Title.

QL776.C66 2003   j591.59   C2002-904293-3

6 5 4 3 2 1   Printed in Canada   03 04 05 06 07

Why Animals Show Off

Peter Cook ~ Laura Suzuki

&

Ron Broda

Scholastic Canada Ltd.

Toronto New York London Auckland Sydney
Mexico City New Delhi Hong Kong Buenos Aires

Who's Who?

A guide to the animals in this book

Animals are listed as they appear on the page, from left to right, unless otherwise noted.

Page 1: northern cardinal

Pages 2-3: common garter snake, American copper underwing, eastern cottontail rabbit, red-breasted nuthatch, duck (in flight), Kirtland's warbler, ruffed grouse, mourning dove, white-tailed deer and doe (above), common snail, northern cardinal (male), American woodcock, barred owl, northern cardinal (female), grey squirrel, northern flicker

Pages 4-5: fire salamander (at top), sea slug, strawberry poison dart frog, blue poison dart frog, harlequin poison dart frog

Pages 6-7: king cobra, porcupine fish

Pages 8-9: (top) viceroy butterfly, monarch butterfly, (top) scarlet king snake, eastern coral snake

Pages 10-11: Malayan pipe snake, peacock butterfly, emperor angelfish, five-lined skink (also called blue-tailed skink)

Pages 12-13: Australian frilled lizard, blue-tongued skink

Pages 14-15: zebra, giraffe, cheetah, tiger

Page 16: (top row) small flambeau, Cairn's birdwing; (second row) common morpho, western pygmy blue, gold-drop helicopis, small harvester; (bottom row) Queen Alexandra's birdwing, orange-barred sulphur

Page 17: (see diagram) 1. brown siproeta, 2. large green-banded blue, 3. common clubtail, 4. large tree nymph, 5. western pygmy blue, 6. Indian leaf, 7. great spangled fritillary, 8. Burmese lascar, 9. orange tip, 10. esmeralda, 11. silver-studded blue, 12. broad-bordered grass yellow, 13. common Mormon

Pages 18-19: (top row) undulated trigger fish, banner fish, lion fish, marine catfish, sea horse; (bottom row) red fromia starfish, yellow sailfin tang, clown fish

Page 20: (top) quetzal, red-crowned crane, vulturine guinea fowl, indigo bunting, yellow warbler

Page 21: (clockwise from top left) Hawaiian honey creeper, blue macaw, cattle egret, Lady Amherst's pheasant (male), blue jay, golden oriole

Pages 22-23: salmon

Pages 24-25: bird of paradise (female and male)

Pages 26-27: silverback gorilla (male), mandrill baboon, bull moose

The world is a colourful place.

But most of the animals in it aren't very colourful. They try to blend in with plants, rocks and dirt. This helps them hide from other animals.

Then there are the showoffs. They come in bright and flashy colours, and their fur, feathers or fins seem to yell "Look at me!"

If blending in helps animals stay safe, why would they want to be showoffs?

3

Some of the biggest showoffs are poisonous. Their wild warning colours tell other animals, "I'm dangerous! Don't mess with me!" And if there is trouble, the attacker will remember those colours next time, and stay away.

- Some tree frogs and salamanders have very poisonous skin.
- This sea slug eats poisonous anemones. Instead of getting sick, it adds the poison to its soft spines.

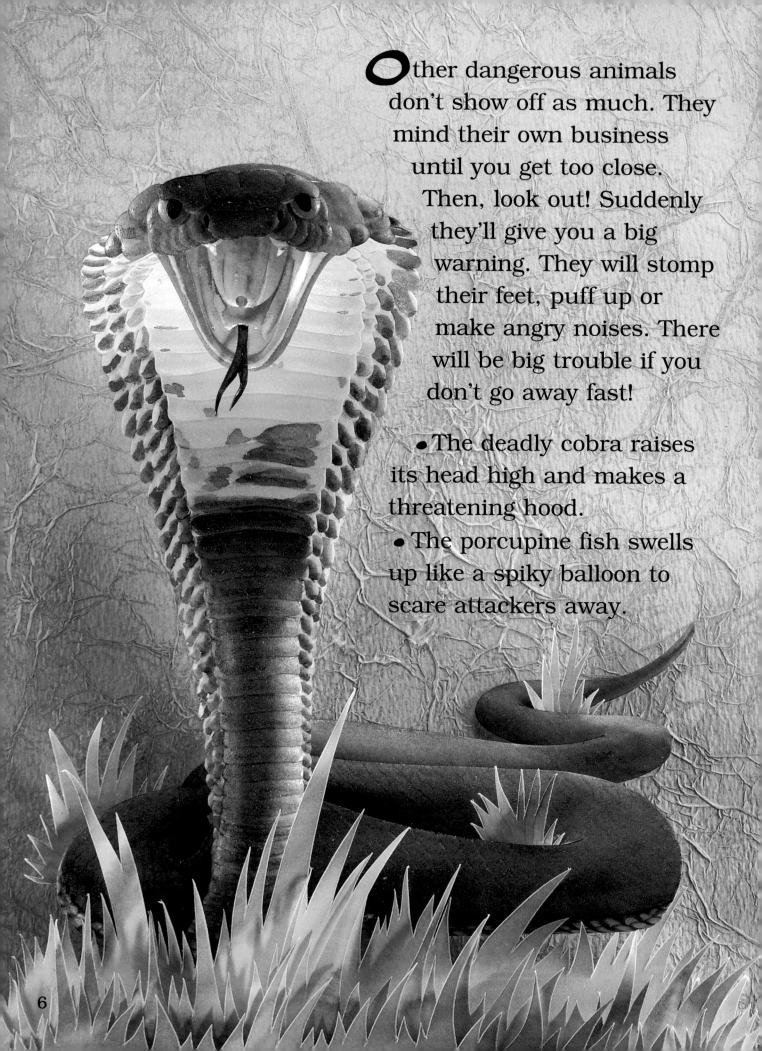

Other dangerous animals don't show off as much. They mind their own business until you get too close. Then, look out! Suddenly they'll give you a big warning. They will stomp their feet, puff up or make angry noises. There will be big trouble if you don't go away fast!

- The deadly cobra raises its head high and makes a threatening hood.
- The porcupine fish swells up like a spiky balloon to scare attackers away.

Bright warning colours work so well that sometimes other animals copy the same colours. These copycats are called mimics.

A mimic isn't dangerous, but it looks a lot like a poisonous showoff. Many attackers are fooled by the mimic's looks. They think the mimic is poisonous, so they stay away.

• The coral snake has a deadly bite. The scarlet king snake (with the red head) doesn't.

• Monarch butterflies eat milkweed, which makes anything that eats them get really sick. But viceroy butterflies (top) are fine for eating.

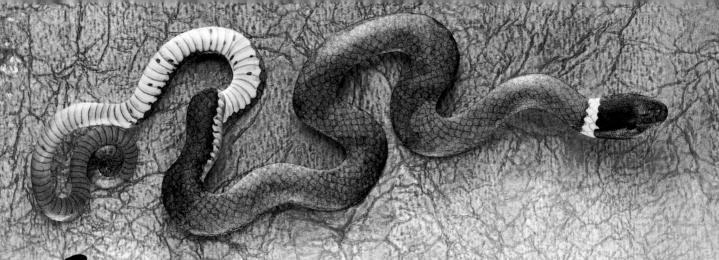

Some creatures show off just one part of their body. An attacker will go for the flashy part, missing the head and other important bits. This gives the animal time to get away.

• The Malayan pipe snake's underside attracts a lot more attention than the rest of its body.

• Some butterflies and fish have showoff spots that look like big eyes, far away from their real head. The peacock butterfly has two sets of fake eyes on its wings.

• The blue-tailed skink's tail will break right off if an enemy grabs it.

Some animals fake it. They don't have a poisonous bite or sting. They try to hide. But when something gets too close, these showoffs suddenly try to look big and fierce. If the attacker is surprised, the showoff gets away. If the attacker isn't fooled, the showoff is dinner.

- The Australian frilled lizard makes itself look scary by opening up a wide flap of skin like an umbrella.
- The blue-tongued skink startles its enemies by sticking out its huge tongue.

Other animals look like showoffs, but they're not.
They seem flashy and colourful to us. But when
you look at these creatures where they live,
their patterns actually help them to blend in.

Big groups of animals with flashy,
swirly patterns can confuse attackers.
This gives zebras a better chance of
getting away.

The stripes and spots on many
animals actually make them
harder to see.

A tiger's stripes help it hide
in the shadows. The spots
on giraffes and cheetahs help
them blend into their
surroundings.

14

All animals need to find others like themselves. Sometimes the only way to do that is to show off and stand out. Insects can be very flashy, and some of the flashiest bugs are butterflies.

In coral reefs, many kinds of fish live together. The fish have different colours and patterns to tell each other apart. These markings let the fish know who is on their team and who is not.

Bright colours help birds figure out who their friends are. These colours help attackers see them, too. But birds can fly away from trouble most of the time.

Animals show off the most when they are looking for mates. That's when they want to be seen. To do this, some fish even change colour, shape and behaviour.

To find mates, some birds show off incredible feathers. The male bird of paradise has a tail so big it can barely fly away from its enemies. Some birds even get caught.

The trick is to be a showoff, but stay alive.

24

Mammals don't usually wear flashy colours. But males still have to show off to prove how big and strong they are. Sometimes they fight, and sometimes they just stamp around a bit. Only the strongest males get to be fathers.

Here's one more flashy animal. People like to show off to say who they are, to warn, to pretend and to belong.